Made in United States
Orlando, FL
26 May 2023

33528702R00063